POLYNEURITIS EQUI EXPLAINED

Siobhan Ellison DVM PhD

Do not go where the path may lead, go instead where there is no path and leave a trail.

—RALPH WALDO EMMERSON

This book is dedicated to veterinarians, horses and their owners that accompanied us on the journey to unravel and uncomplicate polyneuritis equi.

Acknowledgements

Polyneuritis equi is a rare condition seen in horses and because the disease is rare there are few resources that are dedicated to PNE research. Our attempt to reframe the disease using advancements across human and animal medicine, molecular biology, and clinical observations is a complicated task. Almost any of the readers of this book, had they been like minded, could have made the associations that we describe here. Progress in science is made by ordinary clever people building step by step upon the ideas and the work of their predecessors, and our work is no different. The tedious work of creating volumes of standard operating procedures that make certain we meet regulatory standards was accomplished by Debbie Stuart, we are indebted to her efforts. Documenting, reviewing, and updating thousands of case histories were tasks invaluable to our progress, as is our laboratory team, Julie Osborne, Laura Benedetti, and Janis Peterson. We thank Dr David Ellison for his contributions to the text ensuring the words which follow are comprehensible to non-scientists as an essential element in explaining this disease that will ultimately save lives.

Forward

This part is a nontechnical synopsis. It is written for the reader who is not medically trained or someone who wants a simple overview. Our intention is to make information available as widely as possible and still offer the depth of explanation the professional will want. The horse owner will probably want to read the nontechnical parts but may want to delve into the technical parts for more detail.

Advanced Polyneuritis (PNE) is commonly thought of as untreatable so the horse is destroyed. Early recognition and treatment makes recovery likely. If we can educate professionals to recognize the signs and we can provide them the diagnostic tools, we hope to stop the disease before it becomes too late to treat. This is an ongoing process.

Our purpose is to save horses. We have firm scientific data to support what we present here. We are continuing our research. We'll provide the reasons for our conclusions, we'll recommend tests, we'll explain how the tests work and what the tests actually show. We want to refine our understanding as we go forward, we want to improve our detection, and we want to improve treatment. Right now we want to make known the things that will allow veterinarians to save the lives of horses with early disease. If we can do that, we'll save horses.

Polyneurits is rare. It has always been an incurable disease. People don't fund research for rare and incurable diseases. No money means there's been little progress. We have new tools now, these are "molecular tools", we can detect very tiny amounts of substances in the blood and we can tell exactly what they are. If we can find things that shouldn't be there, we can tell what is going on very early, we can know exactly what is causing the early signs, we can intervene, we can stop the damage, we can treat, we can cure. But if the disease is allowed to progress unstopped, to the point that the vital nerve structures are replaced by scar tissue, then indeed it is too late.

If you read the technical parts, you'll see references to "blinded studies". What that means is that the people gathering the data don't know the impact of the data they are gathering. It means they cannot show bias. Suppose you are doing taste tests on colas. If each is in an unmarked glass, you can't know which is which. Your opinions will be honest and unbiased. It's the same way in research. If the vet looking at a lame horse has no idea of how the horse has been treated, he can render an unbiased opinion. They call it being blinded, it has nothing to do with his sight, it has to do with what he's allowed to know when he renders his opinion. You'll also see "placebo" controls. A placebo is essentially a "sugar pill". It is a way to keep people from knowing which animal is actually treated and which isn't. It allows us to tell if the actual pill works better than a sugar pill. Good studies require the participants are not biased. Finally, you'll see "p values". A "p value" just tells you how likely it is that the data is wrong. Commonly we look for a "p value" of "0.05", which is 1/20. That means there's a 95% chance the data is right. It also means there's a 5% chance the data is wrong. Why do we use 0.05? It's because it is a good balance between accuracy and the amount of data needed. Less than 0.05 is generally considered worthless. On the other hand, a study with a 1 in a thousand chance of being wrong could be done, but it may be so expensive no one can do it. With a rare disease, it may be impossible to find enough animals to complete such a study. So now you know what the professionals know, don't let the terms throw you.

You can help with this research. Any animal with even the most subtle signs is important to us. If it is early PNE, we're very interested. If it isn't PNE, that is important to us as well. There are a lot of neurologic diseases, PNE is one of them. It is difficult to tell them apart. Now we have those molecular tools, and they help us, a lot.

CONTENTS

Forward 4
Introduction 7
The Nervous System 10
What is myelin 11
Basic myelin protein P2 14
Inflammation 18
Clinical Signs 19
 Disease 25
Case Analysis 26
Diagnosis 30
Differential Diagnosis 31
Research 34
Polyneuritis revealed 35
Field Studies 40
Your Contribution 41
Diagnostics 45
Testing Options 46

Introduction

Our Purpose

When your horse follows you without being asked, when he rubs his head on yours, and when you look at him and feel a tingle down your spine...you know you are loved.-John Lyons

---

Polyneuritis equi (PNE) is an uncommon neurological disease of mature horses and ponies. Historically, PNE is recognized as untreatable. Unfortunately, veterinarians aren't trained to consider the possibility that polyneuritis equi underlies the clinical signs that can be recognized in horses *before* untreatable disease manifests. Raising awareness about PNE will result in far fewer horses succumbing to life-ending disease. Our purpose is to present these white papers that will inform and educate those interested in PNE.

A white paper is an authoritative report or guide that informs readers concisely about a complex issue. Our white papers present a story that is our hypothesis of PNE. Our papers are meant to help readers understand why disease is difficult to identify and allow a horse owner to grasp the disease process. This information can be used to make decisions for the horse with PNE.

Our white papers weave PNE-relevant results from animal and human research studies and fit the pieces into our current story. Others have a different story without a solution. Our story has a positive ending.

If you are interested in polyneuritis equi, you probably have an afflicted horse or know a person that has a horse suffering from the disease. Polyneuritis equi is rare, less than 50,000 horses a year are diagnosed with PNE. Rare diseases are not well funded and that means little information is generated about them. There are few if any scientists that are conducting studies that will solve the problems including the diagnosis and treatment of PNE.

The information in this book comes from published literature and studies that we conducted. Some of our studies used the most rigorous conditions, the experiments were blinded and placebo-controlled. Some of our studies used cases that were from horses examined by field veterinarians and privately owned. Some field cases could not be used, there just wasn't enough documentation. Using the high FDA-standard of attribution we have over 1700 horses to evaluate over several years. Case reports and collaboration with veterinarians allowed us to generalize in some cases. Often, we had enough data to statistically evaluate some very specific parameters. This body of data moved our work forward. Our work is important because we follow the horses, some of them have been involved for over 5 years. The reports of polyneuritis equi found in the literature come from one or sometimes two cases and that means statistical analysis just isn't possible. Statistical analysis gives the patterns we find credibility.

It is our goal to share our knowledge and bring awareness to this life-threatening disease. We are in the process and will license treatments that can control the clinicals signs of PNE. We are working toward providing a logical strategy to identify and manage disease.

We realize that polyneuritis equi isn't recognized early enough during the onset of disease when it is treatable and possibly reversible. The current dogma surrounding PNE leaves no option other than humane euthanasia because clinical signs that are attributed to this disease only relate to end-stage pathology.

However, polyneuritis equi has an insidious onset. Horses present with subtle clinical signs that can be transient. The clinical signs will reappear and when they do, they are worse. *A defining characteristic of PNE is progressive disease*. When clinical signs are recognized early enough the horse has treatable disease. Perhaps the disease process can be halted with no long-term degeneration. Frustratingly, early signs of PNE are associated with other diseases and that makes diagnosis of PNE difficult. Examining the cellular and molecular aspects of PNE gives us hope that we will achieve our goals.

This book is organized into stand-alone sections. *The nervous system* is an exceedingly brief introduction of the structural element that is needed to understand PNE-and that is myelin. This section explains the molecular structure of myelin because this is where disease happens.

Inflammation is the process of disease and in this section, we relate the process of inflammation to *Clinical Signs*. The section on *Disease* connects the classic and accepted clinical signs of PNE when assessing a PNE horse. *Diagnosis* is the section that reviews and presents a *Differential Diagnosis* list, diseases that are considered in horses with neurological disease. *Research* is a roadmap through the discoveries that brought us to our current thinking about PNE. *Field Studies* explains how you can be involved in polyneuritis research. The *Diagnostics* section reviews a clinical scoring system we propose. This section explains why myelin protein antibodies figure prominently in our diagnostics and provides testing options.

Beau Jackson during happy times in 2015. He is still teaching us about chronic disease.

The Nervous System

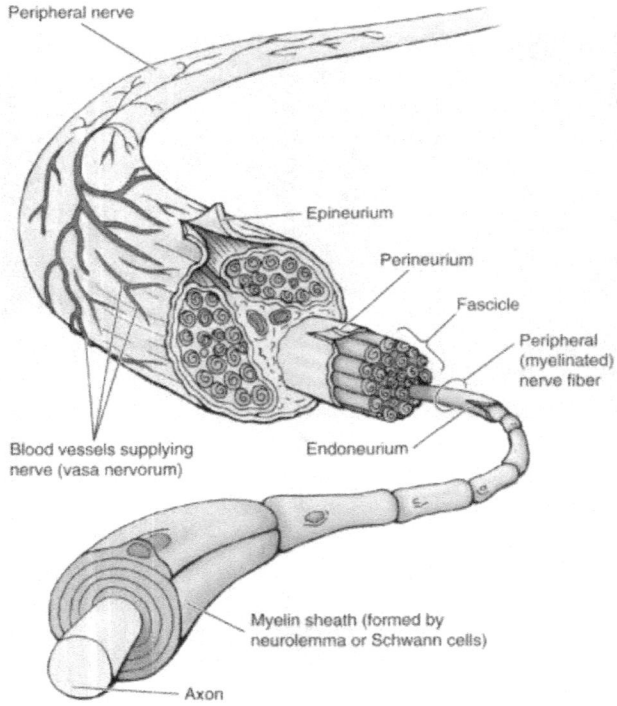

What is myelin

And why is it important

You have brains in your head. You have feet in your shoes. You can steer yourself in any direction you choose.
—Dr Seuss

For this we need some background. When we think of the nervous system, we generally think of two parts, first there's the brain, called the Central Nervous System. Then there is the part that passes information to and from the brain. We call this the Peripheral Nervous System.

Nerve impulses from the body are passed along nerves by shifting chemicals. It is a slow process. Some nerves are fine with slow impulses, the nerves that cause your intestines to move food along, for instance. Then there are the nerves that must pass information very quickly.

Imagine placing a hand on a hot stove. It wouldn't do for the information to take a long time to get to the brain then a long time for the brain to communicate to the muscles to move the hand. The quicker the better. To do that, the fast nerves have a method to move the impulses quickly down a nerve. What happens is that the nerve is insulated with a sheath, this allows the impulse to rapidly skip down the nerve jumping long distances across the insulated portions. This insulation is called a myelin sheath.

If the myelin sheath doesn't work properly, the nerve impulses don't go quickly. This makes the myelin sheath extremely important. To coordinate complicated actions such as walking, running, and chewing, for example, muscle groups need to work in complex coordinated patterns. Each muscle or set of muscles needs to contract in the proper sequence and exactly on cue. Any interruption or delay has severe consequences.

So, animals and people have these important rapid transit nerves. Unfortunately, this myelin sheath can be damaged. Generally, it is the body's own defense system that attacks this myelin sheath. It's the same defense system that helps you conquer disease, and ward off infections. The body has a way of defining what is part of the body, named "self", and what doesn't belong, "non-self" which includes invading bacteria, virus, or protozoa. The body routinely attacks any "non-self" invaders and destroys them.

This "self" identification system is usually perfect. Not always, though. If the body misidentifies something that should be "self" as "non-self", the body attacks the "non-self" with all the resources it has available. In general, it's the immune system. There's also the inflammatory system which works hand in hand with the immune system to destroy invaders.

So how can this happen?

The body breaks down the invaders into small pieces. The body identifies each of these pieces, classifies them as "non-self" and produces antibodies against these pieces. This way the body can wipe out the invaders by attaching antibodies at many places. Think of an antibody like a hook. Each antibody is very specific and only attaches to the piece that it is meant to attack. The body produces a vast number of these antibody hooks. If the target piece exists, the antibody hooks automatically attach and the rest of the immune system uses these hooks to help destroy the invaders.

Now suppose the system that determines "self" and "non-self" gets mixed up. Suppose an invader doesn't get classified as "non-self". The body will not recognize it as an invader and will not attack it. Some bacteria will take advantage of this, they'll coat themselves with materials that the body doesn't recognize as foreign. Parasites sometimes do this as well. The other side of it is that if the body misinterprets what should be "self" as "non-self", those antibody hooks will attach to normal tissue and the immune system will attack it.

This can happen with myelin. There are several ways myelin is misidentified. Once it is recognized by the immune system the processes are set in motion damaging the myelin sheaths. When that happens, myelin fragments are released into the blood stream. We can test the blood to see if those fragments set off reactions in the body. If the blood markers are present, we know that there is a problem.

Suppose one has a horse and that horse develops a coordination problem. Suppose it doesn't walk well, it staggers and falls. If we test the blood and find the myelin fragment markers, that goes a very long way toward telling us why the horse has a problem.

If myelin is attacked by the immune system, all the myelin may be attacked. We won't generally see a single, localizing sign, we'll see an array of signs-diffuse over the body. We call this array of signs polyneuritis. "Poly" means many, neuritis means the nerves are affected. If we're talking about a horse, we tack on the word "equi" so we know we're talking about the horse.

Eli helped us with the diagnosis of neuroinflammatory disease, we've known him for 5 years. He is happily retired and lives in South Florida.

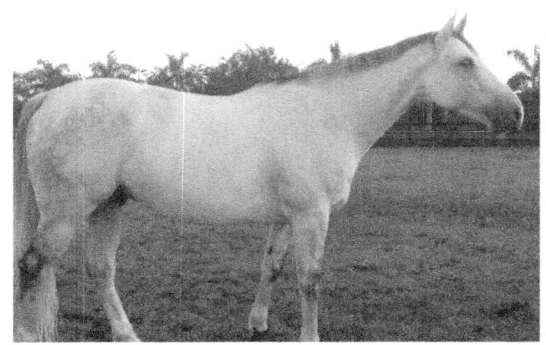

Basic myelin protein P2

And a neuritogenic peptide

"Sometimes the questions are complicated and the answers are simple.".
—*Dr Seuss*

The nervous system is composed of a central and peripheral system. The peripheral nervous system is the part of the nervous system that consists of the nerves and bundles of nerve cells on the outside of the brain and spinal cord. A picture is worth a thousand words, look at the picture in the Inflammation section and let's fast forward to myelin. Myelin is made of proteins, amino acids are the building blocks of proteins. Groups of amino acids are called peptides, peptides can be as small as two amino acids.

Myelin insulates axons, the axon is a long threadlike part of a nerve cell along which impulses are conducted from the cell body to other cells. If myelin, made up of proteins, is damaged then messages are not transmitted to cells. Myelin proteins are highly similar, conserved between species. And that is important to the study of polyneuritis equi (PNE).

When scientists (primarily the English and French) were investigating all manner of neurodegenerative diseases in people they got huge amounts of myelin from the spinal cords of cows because all animals have the same protein structure for myelin. This phenomenon is called conservation. Unfortunately, in 1984 an English cow developed strange signs, the disease turned out to be the first recognition of Mad Cow disease.

Let's digress, I like this part of history and what it gave us. The source of Mad Cow disease was animal feed. Specifically, animal feed contaminated with bits of protein called "prions". First, disease was linked to sheep--but now some believe human bone might have gotten into the British animal feed. Doctors Alan and Nancy Colchester write that Indian and Pakistani peasants sometimes gather large bones from land and rivers to sell, and that "Hindus believe that it is essential for their remains after death to be disposed of in a river, preferably the Ganges. The ideal is for the body to be burned, but most people cannot afford enough wood for full cremation."

During the 1960s and 1970s, the U.K. got a lot of raw material for fertilizers from Bangladesh, Pakistan, and India. Humans were known to have Creutzfeldt-Jakob disease, the infection passed to cows through ground-up bones in animal feed, and then the cows gave it back to people. Fearful of Mad Cow scientists turned to the horse as a source of tissue for their research. This sea of knowledge from horse tissue gave us a leg up on understanding polyneuritis equi.

There were some distinct differences in the equine protein and the bovine protein. Equine myelin is molecularly heavier because it has 3 more amino acids. Ok big deal, I'm being thorough. One unexpected observation was that horses have more, much more, basic myelin P2 protein (let's call it P2) in their central nervous system tissue. And P2 protein makes up 2-15% of the peripheral nervous system protein. The amount and distribution of P2 is a big deal because disease affecting this protein will be more apparent in horses. It was still important that polyneuritis in people could be investigated using equine myelin.

Myelin P2's function is in lipid transport and storage in the cell responsible to myelinate nerves. It was possible to test these myelin making cells (Schwann cells) for damage in polyneuritis. The scientists asked: "Was the cells inability to make myelin the disease process operating in human disease?" If Schwann cells are damaged myelin production would measurably decrease.

Progressive neurological disease was induced in experimental animals by injecting myelin protein. This was important because a model using laboratory animals allowed controlled experiments. An animal model for Guillian-Barre syndrome, a demyelinating disease of the human peripheral nervous system, was produced by injecting P2. If Schwann cells are damaged, myelin production would decrease measurably in the model animals. Myelin production was not altered, new myelin was being produced, indicating that the damage was to myelin.

It wasn't long before a connection was made to neuritis of the cauda equina, now called polyneuritis equi, a neurodegenerative disease in horses. Another similarity between Guillian-Barre and experimental P2 neuritis was paralysis of the trigeminal and facial nerves. Cranial nerve involvement was also recognized in horses.

As an aside, this work was going on in 2005, some purified myelin protein became available. Horse neurologists got some purified spinal protein and injected it into a few horses. But they didn't get disease. **Case closed**. No more work on cauda equina induction by myelin protein. This small experiment closed the door to a model and produced a bias against this line of research that continues today. Did they use P2? And as we explain, different amino acid segments of myelin P2 can cause different signs and outcomes in laboratory animals.

Back in Europe scientists purified equine myelin P2 and crystallized the protein giving them a highly refined molecule. There was another unexpected result of the P2 experiments that may relate to the small horse study. Myelin P2 was snipped (chemically) into peptides, different peptides and disease depended on the peptides that were used in the experiment. Some peptides did not cause disease whereas the whole purified protein did. The conclusion was that there must be a disease-inducing region of the protein. One peptide caused neuromuscular disease and weakness that would resolve, untreated. Another *neuritogenic* (disease causing) peptide consistently induced disease. Animals could become desensitized to disease-causing injections of the whole protein P2, but not to the neuritogenic peptide.

And, normal animals that were given blood cells (T-cells) from diseased animals (passive transfer) got disease! The disease was produced from immune cells from animals, not the protein itself. This raised several questions, but we're going to cut to the chase. It wasn't a malfunction of the cells that put myelin around axons. The myelinating cells did not change the proteins they made, nor did they change the capacity to remyelinate damaged axons in the face of disease.

What changed was the transfer of sensitized cells to a healthy animal. Researchers found that the sensitized cells induced the production of another protein, *an immunoglobulin-binding protein* **on nerves** *that increased during the clinical deficit*. The net result was an increase in the ability of immune cells to bind nerve cells. The nerve cells became the target of the body's immune system.

What about that neuritogenic peptide? Why was this peptide neuritogenic? The neuritogenic peptide of P2, the myelin protein that wraps around axons, contains an inflammatory receptor that is recognized by the immune system. The receptor participates in inflammatory reactions regulating cells that are involved in cell-to-cell signaling by molecules called *cytokines*.

In health, the neuritogenic peptide of P2 (and P2) are not exposed to the body's immune system. When myelin is damaged and P2 is exposed disease ensues. Clinical signs manifest because the exposed peptides sensitize T-cells that stimulate a protein to bind immunoglobulin and make peripheral nerves a target of inflammation.

George embodies the unique relationship between horse and human. They have been together for 22 years. George is retired living with neuroinflammation in California.

Time for the nontechnical explanation. Let me introduce the players in the upcoming illustration. Schwann cells actually make that myelin sheath. Neurons are simply nerve cells. Neutrophils are white blood cells, part of the immune system. Macrophages are another type of white blood cell. Lymphocytes, these are small white blood cells that produce antibodies. Cytokines are inflammatory substances that attract the white blood cells. DRG neuron is a "dorsal root ganglion", these come straight from the spinal cord. Astrocytes and microglia are structural supporting cells (sort of scaffolding for the nerves).

Central sensitization means that the body becomes "aware" of the sensitization. It is a full immune system response after sensitization, no longer just a local process.
The little "ekg like symbols" are to indicate electrical nerve activity. The big red lightning symbols indicate an attack on those important Schwann cells

The illustration shows the interaction between the various parts of the immune system, how the cytokines help in the attraction of the white blood cells to the Schwann cells, and the chain of events that cause the lymphocytes to become sensitized. Once the lymphocytes become sensitized, they manufacture large amounts of specific antibody. Those antibodies are carried in the bloodstream and will attach to other Schwann cells where the process of destruction continues.

The gray ovals are the myelin sheath. The dorsal root neurons (also called upper motor neurons) are slow neurons so they do not have a myelin sheath. The dorsal root neurons would not be affected by the attack on the Schwann cells. Later the text points out that if the process is interrupted early, the Schwann cells can recover and restore the myelin sheath by remyelination.

If the process continues the tissues are replaced by scarring-a process of healing. Once tissues are scared remyelination cannot occur and the damage is permanent. Fibrosis is another word for scarring. The word points out that fibrin, a very tough tissue, is replacing the Schwann cells. Fibrotic tissue is structural and it replaces the functional tissue. Fibrosis is permanent, the Schwann cells cannot ever return. Fibrosis is a part of the general healing process. It fills in for dead tissue. You've seen it in the skin. After a heart attack, fibrosis fills in the area of the dead heart muscle. If you break a bone, inflammation and fibrosis are an important component in healing of the fracture. In general, fibrosis is an end game event in the healing process. It maintains the structural integrity of the area but the underlying function is lost.

Inflammation

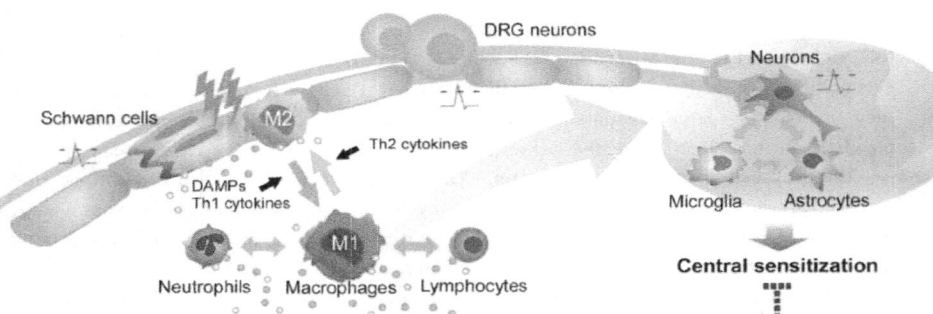

Clinical Signs

Are due to pathology

"You'll miss the best things if you keep your eyes shut."
—Dr Seuss

Some diseases are easy to spot. Unique clinical signs can be directly associated with disease, skin fungus for example. It's hard to ignore your horse when he squints a tearing and swollen eye, those are hallmark signs of a painful corneal ulcer! Fortunately, some diseases have definitive tests. Strep throat is diagnosed with a quick office-run test when kids present with a sore throat. Streptococcus is also diagnosed by a culture in horses suspected of having Strangles.

There are also diseases that aren't so easily recognize. The veterinarian makes a diagnosis by evaluating the clinical signs and narrowing down the possible disease list with an array of laboratory testing. Yet, some difficult-to-diagnose diseases don't have definitive tests to get them onto or off the *differential diagnosis* list.

What can make the definitive diagnosis of some diseases elusive is a fundamental principle: the body reacts to multiple insults by using a few selective, well differentiated pathways. *Innate immunity* is a quick, generic response system and is a first line of defense against infections. A more refined, specific, and later developing response is called *adaptive immunity*. An adaptive response results in specific antibody molecules and sensitized T-cells that are "trained" to recognize a distinct infectious agent. Innate immune responses are non-specific and common to infections while adaptive immune responses are the bodies red flags that may used for a definitive diagnosis.

We are going to explain why polyneuritis equi, that is primarily a dysfunction of the inflammatory response system, can be difficult to recognize. To understand PNE, one must have a brief understanding of how inflammation causes clinical signs.

This section explains the way the immune system normally functions. In polyneuritis the thing that is different is that the immune system is now attacking something it shouldn't. The first step in the immune process is the inflammatory response. Inflammation is a very early response. Even though it is very early it is possible to pick up some nonspecific inflammatory elements in a blood sample. In the PNE disease process abnormal values are associated with subclinical signs. Subclinical means that the signs are generally too subtle to be picked up on a physical exam.

It is important for the body to react quickly to infections. Rapid reactions employed by the innate immune system require communication between several first responding cells to the infection. The blood stream serves as a rapid transit system for the First Responders that are white blood cells (WBC) in innate immunity. These circulating cells are trained in surveillance and at the first encounter with foreign entities they sound the alarm. The signals they use are *cytokines*. Cytokines are chemicals that exert an effect on individual cells and sometimes on tissues.

The immune system is very economical. Sometimes cytokines turn things off and sometimes cytokines turn things on. Cytokines can turn one pathway in a cell on and at the same time turn off a pathway in the same cell. Think of a switching station along a railroad, pulling one lever changes the destination of the train to a meeting in New York or a party in Florida. Knowing when to pull the lever is important and that is *context*. Cytokines receive *context* from other reactions and other cells that let the immune response know where the party is happening.

Innate immune (early and quick) reactions start with inflammation. The five hallmark signs of inflammation are heat, pain, redness, swelling, and loss of function. These signs occur on a large, gross, as well as a microscopic or cellular level. The current discussion focuses on cellular reactions responsible for the gross signs seen in the horse. Inflammation yields changes in measurable clinical laboratory values that may help with a diagnosis of inflammation. Remember that these early, acute reactions are not specific to a specific disease but the response to infection.

Initially, subtle microscopic changes set in motion by cytokines have no outward effect on the horse. The effect is sub-clinical. Yet the ability to measure very minute amounts (or in some cases changes in amounts) of cytokines are accomplished in the laboratory. As the effects of cytokine reactions progress to larger areas of tissues the clinical signs will be noticeable in the horse.

Horses with PNE usually have normal WBC counts. Testing for specific antibodies against bacteria and protozoa will often be negative. Antibody against myelin P2 protein can be absent (early) or present (during fulminant disease). The following discussion will explain why *when* you test and the *context* of testing are important for diagnosis and perhaps prognosis of PNE.

End-stage disease, when a horse is beyond help, is where the current recognition of PNE stands. We want to change that. Late in disease, a transrectal ultrasound scan may show swelling of the sacral nerves as they exit the ventral sacral foramina. A biopsy of the *sacrocaudalis dorsalis lateralis* muscle was useful in one published case. In this case, the horse had no feeling in the tail (clinical signs were paresis or paralysis of the tail and decreased sensitivity). A biopsy showed that WBC's had infiltrated the tissues and obliterated the nerve structure, but not the muscle fibers. Even in this end-stage case an attempt at healing myelin was observed. In some areas that were examined under the microscope, there was new myelin but in other areas, *damaged nerves were covered with fibrotic tissue, the process of fibrosis*.

Fibrosis is interesting, it is the body's attempt to cover nerves that have lost nerve-insulating myelin due to chronic inflammation. The body can remyelinate nerves if inflammation is turned off, but if the repair process is thwarted by chronic inflammation, fibrosis takes over. Myelin allows rapid conduction of messages through the nerve whereas fibrin does not. The clinical signs will not respond to any treatment in late-stage disease when nerves are fibrosed. The *antibody response to myelin* may be absent because the reactive areas of the nerve are covered by fibrosis. The net results is a horse may produce an overabundant amount of granulation tissue that potentiates instead of controls the inflammatory reaction.

Observing remyelination in the presence of inflammation is good news, if fibrosis hasn't occurred. Depressing the initial inflammatory reaction may reverse the clinical signs of disease. The propensity of the horse to have inflammation may be an anatomical difference in this species because horses have significantly more myelin P2 than other species.

A more in-depth view of the process of disease rests in the type of cells that are responding. Inflammatory T-cells and antibody producing cells (CD20+) infiltrate the damaged neural tissues. The infiltrating cells are macrophages (CD11a+ and c+), immunoreactive CD8+, cytotoxic T-lymphocytes, and a few CD4+ helper T-lymphocytes and CD3+ T-cells.

The bottom line is *histopathology supports an adaptive immune response to inflammation* caused by virus, chronic protozoal exposure, rickettsial infections, and immune-mediated diseases. We're not the first ones to ask if PNE is a result of multiple etiologies that set the immune system into motion via common pathways.

PNE was described in the literature (medical books and journals) a long time ago. There are other things that can look like PNE to the clinician examining a horse with neurologic deficits. Many of the published reports were written before the development of the sensitive molecular tools we have today. There were no diagnostic tools to differentiate PNE from some of the other causes of neuromuscular disease. This meant the reports sometimes muddled the various findings. This in no way means the reports weren't good, they were. The books and the papers are not wrong, they're just outdated or incomplete. They don't include the precision with which we can define the disease today. Still, a lot of their findings are valuable. Remember that PNE had no cure and it was often diagnosed late in the disease process. The changes were end stage disease that were found by microscopic examination after an animal was destroyed.

Some published reports cite the involvement of tissues encasing the cerebellum and cerebral hemispheres, although most agree the disease involves the peripheral nervous system and not the central nervous system. In chronic PNE the branches of trigeminal nerves show lesions, again infiltration by inflammatory cells and perineural fibrosis. The spinal column can show reddening and swelling with peridural edema. Lymphocytic infiltrations can be present in various nerves, the femoral nerve or cranial nerves. Horses with long-term disease can also have calcification of spinal nerve roots and extensive perineural fat. The results of these lesions are paresis or paralysis, sensitivity, muscle wasting, gait anomalies, tripping, and dropping feed.

When researchers attempted to find the causes of PNE, it was difficult. It's a rare disease. They looked for infections and signs of trauma. Recall that in the past, at the time of diagnosis, PNE was already advanced. If there was an infection that started the process, that infection was already cleared by the immune system, long before the late signs of PNE appeared. There are other causes of nerve demyelination. Since PNE is the result of the immune response, it doesn't matter too much what sets innate immunity into motion. It matters that the immune system has "seen" the myelin and now sets out to destroy it.

Normally reactive myelin P2 exists inside the Schwann cells membrane. The macrophages (white blood cells) exist in the blood. The myelin P2 is not exposed to the blood stream, so the immune system doesn't know it is there. That's the way it is supposed to work. What can happen, though, is that there's a disruption in the normal Schwann cells integrity and the myelin P2 is exposed to the bloodstream resulting in inflammation. Let me digress for a moment.

This next part is a massive oversimplification of the immune system and its development. Things are far more complicated and involved, and this is only to give you an idea. There is a time in development when the immune system is not "patterned" yet. It is just an early immune system and it has not recognized yet what is normal (called "self") and what shouldn't be there (non-self). Then there's a period when the immune system actively eliminates all the parts of itself that can attack "self". The result is the healthy immune system that ignores all normal tissue, but quickly recognizes anything that should not be there. The trouble is that some parts of the body are hidden from the immune system at the time of this patterning. In general, the bloodstream needs to be in contact with a tissue to recognize "self". All is well as long as that hidden tissue remains hidden.

Now suppose the tissue responsible for keeping that tissue hidden is disrupted. The immune system sees that previously hidden tissue for the first time and it responds the way it always does: attack. The problem isn't that the immune system is acting in a way it shouldn't, it's reacting normally to what it sees as something it didn't see during the "patterning" period. Previously concealed tissue is classified by the immune system as non-self and gets attacked just like everything else that is seen as "non-self". It gets worse. Antibodies produced against invaders don't stop at the limits of the bloodstream, they cross tissues. Now that this tissue has been identified as "non-self", and massive antibody production starts, the antibodies can identify other cells that are hiding similar tissue. Once the antibody hooks on to the tissue, the rest of the immune system goes after it. So, a small area of exposure of a previously hidden "self" tissue can start an immune reaction that attacks all that tissue whether still hidden or not. We see PNE as a disease of a normal immune system attacking normal tissue. Once the hidden tissue is exposed, it doesn't matter so much what started it. Was it trauma? Was it an infection, a virus? It doesn't matter. We think it is innate immunity responding with inflammation. All that matters is that the previously hidden tissue has been "seen" by the immune system and that tissue is now fair game for the immune system.

There's more. When a white blood cell attacks an invader, it engulfs it. The invader is killed then it is systematically broken down into small parts. Those small parts are then released and "shown" to the white blood cells responsible for initiation of antibodies. The lymphocyte has one purpose, that of manufacturing a lot of a single antibody. Lymphocytes are produced with the sole purpose of creating antibodies to one of these bits of that invader. And it isn't just a few lymphocytes, it's a lot of them, the lymphocytes produce large amounts of antibody to that one fragment, and other lymphocytes produce antibodies to other fragments of the invader.

Now a specific antibody latches on to that fragment wherever it finds it. Other invaders that have that same fragments will have antibodies attaching to those fragments. The antibodies, remember they are like hooks, are a molecule for the white blood cells to grab on and engulf that invader. The first invaders are broken down and used as a pattern so that all the same invaders are attacked. And the problem. Once in a while one of those invader fragments will have a *similar pattern* to a part of a normal tissue. The antibody is generally very specific, but if the "self" tissue has a site that is nearly identical to the invader fragment, then the antibody can attach to the normal tissue. When that happens, the immune system will start the inflammatory process involving that "self" tissue. The antibody may not adhere perfectly, after all it was made for a specific part of an invader, but cross reactivity can be a problem, and it can contribute to a class of diseases called "autoimmune diseases". Again, this is just an overview, and we apologize to those that make the immune system their life work.

The differential diagnosis of PNE reviewed the speculations as to the etiology of polyneuritis equi. The problem is that the disease isn't reproduceable using organisms or trauma. By the time chronic inflammation sets in the body has exterminated the organisms sometimes leaving only the residual antibody responses.

Polyneuritis equi is a primary demyelination disease. Primary demyelination can occur without inflammation, this can occur in lead poisoning. Primary demyelination can occur with inflammation where the inflammatory cells are mainly lymphocytes and macrophages. Inflammatory demyelination is thought to have an autoimmune pathogenesis, but the reaction isn't necessarily against "self". We discussed the up-regulation of certain antibody binding areas on myelin P2 as a response to T-cell stimulation in another section.

It was proposed that antigens, or "self"-proteins that reach the peripheral nervous system attract and activate lymphocytes and macrophages. These cells become a nonspecific cause of a primary or even secondary demyelination. This is called a "bystander" mechanism. Finding an infectious cause of PNE is unexpected in this scenario.

It is apparent from the discussion that two processes may be at play. There is an innate immune response that is a quick inflammatory defense against infections. The infection can be a bacterium, a virus, or a protozoan. After the acute phase reaction, the body equilibrates, and the cytokines facilitate a robust adaptive immune response. Normally, acute inflammation switches off while an adaptive reaction is switched on, a cytokine success.

Occasionally the acute inflammatory reaction *doesn't* turn off. It becomes dysregulated. The cytokines forget context and keep the acute reaction in play. The reaction becomes chronic. The cytokines and their end-products keep the reactions going in an endless cycle. As chronic inflammation (T-cells) continue to destroy myelin an adaptive reaction against "self"-myelin ensues. At this point anti-myelin P2 antibodies are measurable.

It is important to recognize where in the cycle the disease is manifesting. We do that by measuring an acute phase cytokine, *C reactive protein* (CRP), and adaptive reactions against two areas of myelin P2. The cytokine CRP is one "turn-on" signal for acute inflammation.

To recap here, a horse will have clinical signs and acute inflammation, elevated CRP and no measurable P2 antibody and it is treatable. As disease progresses a little more, we measure antibodies against whole myelin P2. Further along, with more progressive disease, the horse may become refractory to the whole P2 protein, those antibodies decline, and only the T-cell stimulating protein antibodies (*neuritogenic peptide*) linger, most horses are still treatable and need management. Once the body fibroses damaged nerves and myelin is no longer exposed, the the antimyelin P2 antibodies decline. Nerves can't conduct signals yielding clinical signs that are progressively worse. And the horse is untreatable.

Jazzy uses a raked arena to demonstrate subtle signs that are rear limb toe dragging, rear limb weakness and a wide based stance.

Disease

Case Analysis

Measuring Disease

"How did it get so late so soon?"
—*Dr Seuss*

A case report is a method we use to document clinical signs in a horse with polyneuritis equi. Comparing multiple reports are a useful tool for the veterinarian and horse owner. The change in **Clinical Score**, over time, is used to track the progression of disease. We developed a **Case Analysis Form** to analyze cases of suspected polyneuritis equi using the same process. You can use our question-based form, find it at http://pathogenes.com/w/case-analysis/ to evaluate a case of your own. The information provided by the Case Analysis is statistically useful and can add to our knowledge database.

In *Case Analysis* we review the clinical signs of PNE. An analysis of the few published reports of PNE using our Case Analysis Form demonstrate the utility of the form. These six cases, along with clinical experience, are the current basis of understanding of PNE. The few published cases were untreatable, and the horses were euthanized. We discuss our own data set, derived from a disease-induction model, the statistical incidence of signs that we provide may be beneficial to field veterinarians. Finally, a summary of over a thousand field cases is insightful and instructive for recognizing horses with suspected polyneuritis equi.

We grouped clinical presentations into six groups of signs that make sense to us. Each group is scored for severity, a score of 0 is given to a clinically normal horse. A score of 1 means the signs are mild, a score of 2 indicates the signs are moderate, and a score of 3 is assigned to severe signs. Noting the duration of signs matters because signs appear sequentially in experimentally induced disease and progressive signs may also be sequential in natural disease.

The idea that there is a predisposition for the involvement of the extradural nerve roots of the cauda equina gave *cauda equina syndrome* its name. The *cauda equina* anatomically describes the bundle of nerves below the end of the spinal cord. People with cauda equina syndrome have symptoms of low back pain, pain radiating down the leg, numbness around the anus and loss of bowel or bladder control. Horses also show sensitivity, numbness, and paresis or paralysis. Pain in horses is recognized by tail rubbing. Pain may be appreciated if the horse avoids being touched or a muscle trembles when it is palpated.

The name polyneuritis equi was adopted when a clearer understanding of disease pointed to a more diffuse distribution of signs in horses. Mature horses and ponies of both sexes get polyneuritis equi. Measuring antibody against two different reactive areas of myelin protein may allow us to stage disease, an important step in developing a prognosis. We determine the immune response to the whole P2 protein and MPP (neuritogenic peptide) and discuss the relevance to clinical cases in the section *Diagnostic Testing for PNE*.

Polyneuritis equi is progressive and initially, subtle. Natural and experimentally induced cases have a regional change in skin *sensitivity*, decreased *muscle tone, paresis or paralysis* of muscles, *muscle atrophy or muscle fasciculations, gait anomalies*, and sometimes, *cranial nerves signs*.

Animals become sensitive to touch. A section of our case analysis addresses **SENSITIVITY**. Increased sensitivity is called hyperesthesia that can predominate or it can be missed. As the disease progresses the responses to touch are decreased, a decrease in sensation is called hypoesthesia. The discomfort, perhaps a pins-and-needles like feeling, manifests as rubbing the tail. By the time PNE is considered, sensitivity associated with the tail and anal sphincter are decreased and muscle tone may be decreased. The perianal region shows decreased sensitivity as do the muscles along the back (epaxial), gluteal, semitendinosus and semimembranosus muscles. The prepuce is not affected, the nerves supplying the perineum and penis are separate from the innervation to the prepuce. The "fly-twitch" muscles show an abnormal sensitivity, increased or decreased, and is called the *panniculus response*.

MUSCLE TONE is an important parameter to assess when considering polyneuritis equi. The tongue, anus, perianal region, tail, bladder or urethral sphincter can have an abnormal, decreased or absent muscle tone.

Muscles can show **PARESIS OR PARALYSIS**. Classically, muscles associated with the penis, urinary bladder, or tail are abnormal. Horses can dribble urine or show abnormal urination. Horses may have cystitis, a urinalysis with culture is worthwhile. An abnormal tail carriage, holding the tail to one side, is present in some horses with PNE. Horses can have difficulty eating (dysphagia) or excessively drop feed. Muscles of mastication, the face, or tongue can be paretic-some horses can't move the bolus of chewed food from the cheek in a process called "quidding". Horses can show abnormal swallowing. Muscles of the rectum can be involved, and horses may retain feces. Pelvic limbs can be weak resulting in mild ataxia.

Often there is **MUSCLE ATROPHY OR FASCICULATION**. There can be a loss of muscle mass along the topline, the epaxial muscles, making the horse appear thin. Also, the gluteal, semitendinosus, semimembranosus, muscles used for chewing (masticatory muscles), facial and tongue muscles can show atrophy. Muscle trembling, fasciculation, can be observed in any muscles but frequently fasciculation of supporting muscles is observed when a rear limb is elevated. A blacksmith may comment on this sign weakness when lifting the rear leg to trim the foot.

GAIT ANOMALY'S most often reported as proprioceptive deficits but can be a weakness appreciated using the tail pull test. Some horses are reported to show ataxia, although ataxia is more often associated with spinal nerves while PNE is thought to involve peripheral nerves until very late-stage disease. As disease extends to affect the nerve roots supplying the gluteal, sciatic, and femoral nerves horses will become ataxic.

CRANIAL NERVE SIGNS are observed by a change in behavior, the most commonly reported sign in our database. Vestibular signs are associated with vestibular nystagmus (movement of the eye latterly) or overall weakness. A head tilt or an eye drop when the head is elevated are also signs of vestibular disease. Owners often report the lips are drooped to one side, the lips twisting to the unaffected side.

Six published, end-stage cases (Aleman 2009, Rosseaux 1985, van Galen 2008) are available to evaluate with our Clinical Scoring system. We show the Clinical Score for each group of signs. All the cases reported a 2 for Sensitivity. Muscle tone signs were the most severe in Aleman's case, moderate in the 2 cases reported by Rosseaux, and absent in the three cases reported by van Galen. Paresis or paralysis was moderate in all the cases except the Aleman report, that horse was mild for this category and is the only report of muscle atrophy or fasciculation. Gait deficits were reported in 4 of the six cases, mild for Aleman and one of Rosseaux horses and moderate for one Rosseaux horse and one van Galen horse. Cranial nerve involvement was present and moderate in four horses and absent in Aleman's and one Rosseaux horse.

Polyneuritis-like signs were induced in 75 horses in placebo controlled, blinded studies. The horses were scored by clinical examinations conducted by equine veterinarians certified by the American College of Veterinary Internal Medicine. The observed signs were associated with inflammation. Clinical signs appeared at 10 days in some horses and progressed over the 120 days of the studies. One horse experienced a seizure. Surprisingly, horses with induced disease showed *consecutive* clinical signs, although the duration of each stage varied between individuals. The sequential timing of signs relates to the pathogenesis of disease possibly tracking the path of inflammation by anatomy in the diseased horse.

Diseased horses dropped feed, drooled, and their lips were slack, or twisted to one side. Facial muscle paresis and muscles of mastication were next to show disease. Some horses had a droopy eyelid and most had behavior changes that were apparent early during the progression of disease. Horses would lose position in the herd and one horse became dangerously aggressive.

A parked- out stance and laying down more frequently were signs of weakness. All horses showed slight epaxial muscle wasting and hyposensitivity. A curious adaptive behavior was adopted by 6 horses housed in one paddock. The horses would cluster very close together, perpetually in motion around the paddock; their tails atonic and panniculus reflex absent- they were defenseless against vicious biting flies. The abnormal behavior resolved immediately when they were treated for flies.

Muscle wasting along with abnormal proprioception developed a little later. A transient laryngeal hemiplegia (respiratory nerve dysfunction) presented in 40% of horses and may suggest horses with suspected disease should undergo endoscopy.

The order of appearance of clinical signs in experimentally induced disease and the percent of horses showing a sign (in the grouped signs) were: paresis/paralysis (81%); muscle tone (78%); cranial nerve signs (84%); gait anomaly-predominantly weakness (73%); sensitivity (54%). And finally, muscle atrophy that was present in 30% of the research horses. These horses were diseased for 120 days and only one was so severely afflicted that it was euthanized.

Our analysis of more than a thousand horses reveals one commonality. And that is serum antibody against myelin protein P2 is present. The key signs reported by veterinarians on clinical exam that raise our suspicion about PNE are a chronic history of disease, behavior, gait anomalies (proprioceptive deficits), muscle atrophy, and abnormal sensitivity.

Jazzbehavingbadly.

Diagnosis

Differential Diagnosis

Neuroinflammatory diseases

"From there to here, from here to there, funny things are everywhere!"
—Dr Seuss

A **differential diagnosis** is the process of distinguishing one disease or condition from others that present similar signs. Differential diagnostic procedures and tests are used by veterinarians to diagnose the specific cause (etiology) of disease in their patient, or, at least, to eliminate any imminently life-threatening conditions. Several diseases look like polyneuritis equi (PNE). Also, PNE is an uncommon and overlooked disease that may have many etiologies. We think it deserves be considered in horses with neuromuscular disease.

Diagnostic testing is used to pare down the disease-causing possibilities. A bottom up approach to diagnosis starts with a good history and clinical evaluation to document the clinical signs. There are studies that collect epidemiology data and define risk factors for some diseases. Epidemiology data helps when evaluating the neurologic horse because different etiologies, that use common host-response mechanisms, yield similar signs. Some diseases are quickly ruled out based on epidemiology. Disease may be more prevalent in certain breeds or ages thus the signalment is important. Evaluating the clinical signs is the first step to diagnosis. Comparing clinical signs over time is useful information when considering a diagnosis of PNE.

Disease processes affecting the nervous system may be congenital or familial, infectious or inflammatory, toxic, metabolic, nutritional, traumatic, vascular, degenerative, neoplastic, or idiopathic.

Congenital disorders may be obvious at birth or shortly after (underdeveloped cerebellum). Some familial disorders (equine motor neuron disease) cause a progressive degeneration of neurons in the first years of life, whereas others (inherited epilepsy) may not manifest for 2–3 yr.

Infections of the nervous system are due to specific viruses, fungi, protozoa, bacteria, rickettsia, prions, and algae. Noninfectious inflammations such as steroid-responsive meningoencephalomyelitis and meningoencephalomyelitis of unknown etiology and other CNS inflammatory diseases may be immune-mediated. Rabies should always be considered in horses with neuromuscular disease.

Toxicity of the nervous system is most frequently caused by organophosphates, pyrethrins, carbamates, metronidazole, sedatives, and anticonvulsants. Botulinum, tetanus, and tick toxins, as well as coral and certain other snake venoms, cause neurologic signs. Lead can be related to CNS toxicity. Regionally available plants, such as creeping indigo or false dandelion are toxic and cause neuropathies.

Metabolic alterations of nervous system function most commonly result from hypoglycemia, hypoxia or anoxia, hepatic dysfunction, hypocalcemia, hypomagnesemia, hypernatremia, hypokalemia, and uremia. Hypothyroidism, hyperthyroidism, hypoadrenocorticism, and hyperadrenocorticism are endocrine disorders that can cause neurologic dysfunction.

Vitamin E deficiency results in ataxia and muscle wasting. Vitamin E deficiency can be the rare equine motor neuron disease or more common, equine degenerative myeloencephalopathy-the prognosis is different for each of these diseases.

Trauma to the PNS and CNS causes focal and multifocal neurologic signs from physical damage, hemorrhage, edema, and progressive formation of oxygen-containing free radicals and nervous system destruction. Damage from trauma is usually complete in 24–48 hours and the signs will plateau in the horse. Continued degeneration of signs may extend as long as four days because inflammatory cells are slow to infiltrate into damaged tissues.

Vascular lesions of animals are usually due to septicemia and bacterial embolization of the CNS. Fibrocartilaginous embolization of the spinal cord is seen in athletic horses. Arteriovenous malformations occur occasionally and cause spontaneous hemorrhages. Cerebrovascular disease from arteriosclerosis is rare in domestic animals but has been associated with hypothyroidism caused by hyperlipidemia. Cerebrovascular disease due to hypertension is rare but is possible.

Degeneration of neurons occurs in acquired lysosomal storage disorders. Degeneration of intervertebral discs that subsequently herniate into the vertebral canal often produces paresis and paralysis and can be acute.

Neoplasms of the CNS and PNS are most common in dogs and cats but cancers are found in horses. Astrocytes, oligodendrocytes, and microglia can all become neoplastic and form astrocytomas, oligodendrogliomas, and gliomas. Ependymal cells and the choroid plexus, which line the internal cavities of the CNS and produce cerebrospinal fluid, also can become neoplastic and form ependymomas and choroid plexus papillomas. Meningeal cells of the dura, arachnoid, and pial membranes form meningiomas. Neurofibrosarcomas are tumors of the nerve sheaths of peripheral nerves. Lymphosarcoma is a common metastatic tumor of the PNS and CNS in other species.

The idiopathic mechanism of disease is reserved for described syndromes with characteristic clinical signs, predictable outcomes, and no known necropsy findings.

A review of signalment, history, and clinical signs will point to the system involved, in PNE it is the *neuromuscular system*. Polyneuritis equi is a disease that affects the *peripheral* nervous system.

Diseases that have similar presenting signs can impact the *central nervous system* (CNS). The differences between PNS and CNS disease can be subtle and it takes some experience to figure out.

Specific neuromuscular etiologies that commonly affect horses are: *cervical vertebral stenotic myelopathy* (CVM) or *Wobblers Syndrome*. Signs are usually symmetric (central nervous system) with the hind end (pelvic limbs) more affected than the forelimbs. A horse with CVM can have atrophied muscles. It is diagnosed more often in young horses. *Trauma* can cause peripheral or central disease.

Infectious causes of neuromuscular disease include *Herpes virus* due to EHV-1 associated neurologic disease is associated with a respiratory infection and can include a history of fever. Signs are usually symmetric and involve the rear end. Clinical signs include pelvic limb weakness, progressive ataxia, bladder distention without incontinence, decreased sensitivity over the perineal region (hypoalgesia) tail paralysis, and fecal retention. Cranial nerves can be involved, and central signs can include depression. Two infectious causes of neuromuscular disease are *Lyme disease-neuroborreliosis* and *Equine protozoal myeloencephalitis*. These diseases involve the CNS. Rabies should always be considered in an unvaccinated horse with neurological disease.

Horses with *Equine Motor Neuron Disease* show clinical signs of limb weakness and muscle fasciculations and tremors. Muscle atrophy is usually widespread and extreme. This disease can be responsive to Vitamin E therapy. *Equine Degenerative myeloencephalopathy* is not responsive to Vitamin E and has some tight epidemiology parameters.

It is generally accepted that PNE is a peripheral disease. Clinical signs that involve the cranial nerves are evaluated and must be ascribed as affecting the central or peripheral nervous system to rule in or rule out diseases that primarily affect one system or the other. It is confounding that some disease processes involve *both* systems! And it is equally confounding that polyneuritis equi may be recognized as a pathophysiological process that is associated with several etiologies.

This is Katie in 2011, one of our first cases. She has several signs of polyneuritis equi including weakness, ataxia, abnormal tail carriage and muscle wasting.

Research

Polyneuritis revealed

"Think left and think right and think low and think high.
Oh, the thinks you can think up if only you try!"
—Dr Seuss

A well-known parable describes three blind men encountering a strange animal but have no experience with it. It's an elephant, so the story goes. The first blind man touches the elephant's trunk and says, "This animal is like a snake." The second blind man, while touching the elephant's leg, says, "You're wrong. I feel the great trunk of a tree, it isn't an animal at all." The third blind man, touching the side of the massive animal, says, "You both are wrong. I feel a wall." Each of the men thinks he is right, and the others are wrong. But, in fact, they are all describing different parts of the same elephant. Scientists examine novel diseases in much the same way using the tools that are available to them. A difficult to understand disease polyneuritis equi, is much like the elephant encounter.

There are problems with this analogy. The parable assumes the blind men were touching an elephant. We also assume the animals described as PNE in the literature are truly cases of PNE. Classically, clinical signs are the basis for assigning a diagnosis of PNE to a neuromuscular disorder in horses after other more common etiologies are ruled out. The story assumes there was an elephant that had defined characteristics—there were objective realities about the creature that the men were attempting to define according to their finite understanding that would identify it as an elephant. The elephant was not the sum of these three men's descriptions of it but elephants possess definitive attributes apart from these men's speculations. We speculate that polyneuritis equi is a conundrum because PNE shows a spectrum of signs that reflect the characteristics of the pathology over time. It is a syndrome that changes with time. PNE is classically described and defined at the terminal stage and we can all agree on a diagnosis at this stage, the only actionable course is euthanasia. The challenge is recognizing PNE early enough in the inflammatory cycle to make a difference in clinical outcome.

The second problem with the analogy is that it does not allow for contradictory claims about the nature of the elephant. Notice that all three men were touching different parts of the elephant and giving different descriptions of what the elephant was like. But suppose all three were touching the same part of the elephant: the leg. And again, they disagree. Each of these three men may make a claim that contradicts the other two based on their experience. It isn't reasonable that only one of the three men can be correct. Science allows for a comparison of claims if the same conditions for the experiments were used.

We suggest that the overriding clinical sign of PNE is antibody against myelin P2 protein (P2). Yet there are contradictory claims from the Establishment that this test lacks specificity. We disagree. The few researchers in United States that investigated using P2 protein to identify cases of end-stage PNE did not publish their results. They used *whole protein* from spinal cords of horses (personal communication). There were *very few cases* available for their analysis. Attempts were made to *induce disease* in a couple of horses by injecting P2 protein, but this experiment failed to produce clinical signs (personal communication). We found reasons for their failures that resulted in a misunderstanding and lack of recognition of treatable PNE.

Scientists tried to find a causal relationship between diseases such as multiple sclerosis or Guillian-Barre syndrome and *Sarcocystis* more than 65 years ago. Statistically, patients with these autoimmune diseases were *more likely* to have antibody against *Sarcocystis* than clinically normal people, but no hard link was ever made. We investigate molecular inflammatory events stimulated by *Sarcocystis* in horses with neurological disease and find that there may be an association with horses that develop PNE. To figure out why we refined some diagnostic tools and developed others.

Tools that were developed for progressive, autoimmune diseases in people serendipitously benefitted horses. Not long after Mad Cow Disease surfaced equine spinal cord tissues were substituted for cow spinal tissues in studies. This period of research was a P2 revolution. Justifying replacing cow tissue with horse tissue coincided with a surge in the field of molecular biology. The molecular structure of equine myelin P2 protein was elucidated, a model for inducing severe experimental autoimmune neuritis was developed, and the ability of P2 to up-regulate genes targeting peripheral nerves was recognized. A boon to our research was the identification of a disease-causing peptide (MPP) that is a component of P2 and is involved in PNE. This research was accomplished almost thirty years ago.

Ten years before equine P2 experienced its revolution, bovine tissues were used to detect P2 antibodies in four cases of cauda equina neuritis. Human neurologists had turned their attention to naturally occurring disease in horses (called *cauda equina neuritis*) because it was important to compare-and-contrast the induced disease models with naturally occurring disease. Interest in cauda equina neuritis in horses was stimulated by the similarity of Guillain-Barre syndrome and experimental P2 neuritis in rats. The *unequivocal* presence of antibodies to bovine P2 in the tested sera suggested that antibody against myelin played a pathogenic role in PNE. In the early stages of PNE it was possible that nerves showed no macroscopic abnormality, or they were slightly more translucent. Histologically, demyelination and cell infiltration by lymphocytes, plasma cells and macrophages were recognized. As disease advanced, there was fibrous thickening of the tissue that surrounded nerves. Also recognized was that early and advanced lesions may be found in different places in the same nerve or different nerves of the same horse.

In 1984 Muhammed Ali was diagnosed with Parkinson's disease, Michael Jorden entered the NBA draft, Indira Gandhi was assassinated and Canadian clinicians analyzed 2 cases of PNE concluding that horses produce an overabundant amount of granulation tissue that potentiates instead of controls the initial inflammatory reactions. Those insightful veterinarians speculated that if the initial reaction to the inciting antigen (still a decade before P2 research exploded) could be suppressed, the degree of neurological damage would be limited and *may be reversible*, providing that fibrosis hadn't occurred.

A short three years later a promising diagnostic test was developed. London researchers used an enzyme linked immunosorbent assay (ELISA) to detect *all cases of PNE* that had caudal nerve involvement. They reported the test was of limited value in differentiating neuropathies involving only cranial or other peripheral nerves. They found 12 cases of PNE based on clinical or post mortem criteria from 14 seropositive sera. Only one case had a low PNE score, and it was a horse with shivers.

Had contemporary researchers used recombinant proteins or used the neuritogenic peptide (MPP) perhaps their opinion of the utility of serum testing for PNE would be different. Had the database containing detailed and long-term histories of hundreds of horses with neurological disease been available for testing P2 antibodies, as does ours, the dogma would be different today.

The first described cases of cauda equina syndrome indicated that the disease agent has an apparent predisposition for nerve roots as they exit the spinal column, the anatomical location of the cauda equina. The logical name was *cauda equine neuritis* in horses or *cauda equina syndrome* in people. Polyneuritis equi was differentiated from cauda equina neuritis by the presence of cranial nerve involvement in two cases-but now they are thought to be the same condition. Polyneuritis equi (PNE) more adequately describes a diffuse, peripheral inflammatory neuropathy. End stage disease is characterized by progressive, insidious granulomatous inflammation of peripheral nerves.

Two predominant theories, viral and autoimmune, are consistent with the post-mortem findings in tissues from cases of PNE. However, no etiologic agent is consistently found in tissues-- most likely because disease isn't recognized early enough. Rousseaux provided evidence that peripheral neuropathies are likely reversible early in the disease process in 1981. Unfortunately, chronic untreatable disease sets in before it is considered as a diagnosis today. Multiple rounds of inflammation, followed by healing, continues until granulation tissue predominates.

Aleman *et al* reported the presence of B-lymphocytes and plasma cells in one case of suspected PNE, an 8-year-old gelding with dysuria. The presence of antibody producing cells indicate antibodies were being produced in the diseased tissues in this horse. Their findings affirm those of early researchers that the presence of antibodies may be involved in the disease process. Aleman *et al* observed early attempts at nerve regeneration in histology sections of diseased tissues echoing the speculations of past workers: enhancing nerve myelination may be possible, if the inflammatory response was controlled early in the disease process.

Early detection of PNE would require assay's designed to detect inflammation *prior to* the development of the granulomatous inflammatory responses. Granulomatous tissue is the bodies response to chronic inflammation. The fibrotic tissue successfully bandages the damaged nerve and decreases immune responses at the expense of nerve conduction and function. Fibrosis occurs after myelin is exposed and elicits an immune reaction.

Inflammation with loss of function can result in several equine neuropathies. The presence of post-infection pathology results from inflammation associated with Lyme disease (borreliosis), sarcocystosis, and neosporosis. No organisms were ever isolated in respective infection models, however both innate (inflammation) and adaptive immunity (antibody) were elicited by the infections. Centers for Disease Control, CDC, recognizes a post-Lyme disease syndrome that is unresponsive to antibiotics. They realize that inflammation persists after infection and inflammation is the cause of chronic disease, not the persistence of organisms.

Infectious or autoimmune mechanisms are proposed as PNE-inciting pathologies. How about both? It was proposed that infectious agents initiate immune-mediated conditions in some cases of PNE. The damaged nerves expose myelin and horses produce measurable anti-myelin P2 antibodies. Aleman didn't look for circulating P2 antibodies in their clinical case, the gelding was euthanized due to rapid progression of disease and a poor prognosis, a typical outcome for these cases.

The use of P2 to bind antibodies in suspected cases of polyneuritis equi was accomplished by Kadlubowski and a few years later, by Fordyce. Yet, it is generally thought that the test is not specific. An understanding of case recognition and the pathogenesis of PNE may explain why some horses are P2 test positive and some are negative. Presence and detection of circulating P2 antibody may be explained in context of the stage of disease. We suspect horses will test positive early in the process but may test negative when nerves are fibrosed. Fibrosis occurs in late-stage disease and is the condition present in published reports. We detected anti-P2 in horses that did not have end-stage disease.

Rodent models of experimental P2-induced polyneuritis show an initial reaction against the whole P2, this can be expected in horses with early inflammatory PNE. As disease progresses, the activity against P2 could wane if tolerance develops in horses, as it did in rodents. Surprisingly, reactivity against the *neuritogenic peptide* did not diminish in laboratory animals. If this is true in horses, pre-end stage disease that is recognized as classical polyneuritis equi in referral centers may no longer have reactive serum antibodies that would be detected by P2 ELISA, but they would have circulating antibodies against the neuritogenic peptide. We don't expect all horses with fibrotic repair to have circulating antibodies against P2. The time that antibody is present after fibrosis of myelin antibody-stimulating tissue may depend on the individual's response. The collective data from Rostami *et al* demonstrated a cellular response to the neuritogenic peptide and to a lesser extent to P2 protein in rats. This work by Rostami may explain the unpublished observations of researchers in the United States. They assayed for antibody against P2 in end stage disease. A P2-refractory state may be present in the horses they examined. We assay for antibody against both P2 *and* the neuritogenic peptide to suggest a diagnosis of polyneuritis equi.

The proposed pathogenesis of PNE includes the *adaptive response* to an infection. Pick any etiology, it doesn't matter because there is a universal response to infections. The adaptive response includes a signal that turns on a local expression of a protein (for those of you that want all the details, the protein is an immunoglobulin binding protein) that is found on peripheral nerves (expression is up-regulated during the adaptive response) making peripheral nerves a targeted site for inflammatory reactions and resultant damage. There is an inflammatory response. This occurs before the immune cell-binding protein is up-regulated on myelin. The second response is the adaptive responsive and is later during disease. Two responses. The proverbial elephant looks different and the differences depend *when* you look.

The reactive site for experimental polyneuritis is located on the neuritogenic peptide, MPP. This peptide contains a T-cell epitope that can *adaptively transfer* EAN to naïve rats. Adaptive transfer is a process by which T-cells or antibodies (without disease causing organisms) are given to healthy animals to passively transfer immunity. Passive transfer can be useful, a horse or cow transfers protective antibodies to their young in the first milk. The newborn absorbs these immune molecules from its first meal. Adaptive transfer is useful for disease models because disease can be transferred using autoimmune antibodies. Likewise, sensitized T-cells can transfer autoimmune diseases by the adaptive transfer of autoimmune-stimulating cells from an animal that suffers from an autoimmune disease into a healthy animal. This is a model to produce disease.

Results of a molecular analysis of MPP, the T-cell epitope, identified the *equine IL6 epitope*- the cytokine IL6 is an initiator of innate inflammatory reactions. To summarize, the P2 protein has a T-cell epitope, a physical location on peripheral nerves for the cytokine IL6 to exert an effect. By the way, it isn't all together surprising that some sophisticated organisms that want to attract inflammatory cells during infections (*Sarcocystis neurona*, for example) and mimic T-cell epitopes.

When taken together, we suggest that it is possible that horses with PNE develop sensitized T-cells that could transfer disease to naïve horses or naïve rats and serve as a model of this disease. This is a testable hypothesis. Further, the pathology in rats showed that transferring T-cells resulted in increased expression of a gene encoding an *immunoglobulin-binding protein*. This transiently expressed protein is a part of the myelin surrounding nerves and nerve roots and may correlate with increased immune complex binding capacity during maximal clinical deficits.

This hypothetical mechanism of disease, specifically that IL6 mediates a dysregulated inflammatory condition could apply to horses with PNE and may account for increased antibody against P2 and MPP during disease exacerbation. It is evident that there is a major pathogenic role for cytokines, specifically IL6 and IFN-γ in EAN. If a similar disease process is present in horses, specifically blocking cytokine production, would be palliative. Our ongoing studies intended to develop treatments that control the clinical signs of PNE test our hypothesis because therapies target T-cells to treat disease.

Field Studies

Because it isn't always easy to get to a clinic

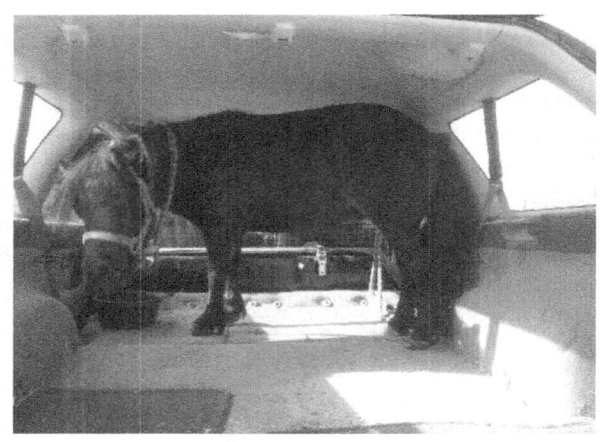

Your Contribution

How you can help

*"Unless someone like you cares a whole awful lot,
nothing is going to get better. It's not."*
—Dr Seuss

We hope you don't have a horse with polyneuritis equi. If you have a horse with suspected PNE, this guide is for you. It is said that *it is an ill wind that blows no man good*...and so it goes that samples and a case history from your PNE-horse can help our understanding of this horrible disease. The data we collect and analyze increases our ability to help other horses. There are two links found at: http://pathogenes.com/w/case-analysis/ The forms are designed to gather the data that is most useful to us. We hope you will use the forms and refine your quest for answers about horses with suspected PNE.

Most veterinarians get new information from the results of studies that are reported in the veterinary literature or at continuing education meetings. The pipeline for dissemination of information can be from 3-5 years. The studies are conducted and discussed by our peers at meetings. The work is then submitted for peer review and finally, publication. Our research is presented at the special information sessions (SIG's) for EPM and published in peer reviewed journals. If you missed the meetings or don't have easy access to the papers, you can find them on our home page http://pathogenes.com/w/

A recent AAEP newsletter quoted Dr. Larry Bramlage as saying "For practicing veterinarians, research is the currency we trade in, and every day we use the information these researchers generate." They recognize the increasing need for research to help find solutions for equine diseases and formed a Foundation. AAEP's research Foundation claims two chief functions: "the leading effort is to support the Foundations efforts to increase donations to fund projects and build an endowment to generate future resources and second, to prioritize areas of need to serve as the focus of future research."

Orphan diseases like PNE are not on the radar. We continue our efforts to run well controlled studies generating information that practitioners can use every day for difficult cases. The funding for our research comes from our consulting services. Supporting our research advances our goals that are to ensure orphan equine diseases become a priority and enter them into the pipeline that will develop better diagnostics and treatments.

Our research goals for PNE are to identify horses that have clinical signs consistent with a diagnosis of polyneuritis equi and prevent them from getting terminal disease. To accomplish these goals, we developed a treatment for PNE and are taking the steps to get FDA licensing that will make treatments commercially available. FDA licensing is important, licensing ensures drugs are labeled for use in horses. Licensing is an expensive process. Our studies are rigorous, controlled, and enlist top tier equine neurologists. Our work resulted in a database that ensures the next step in equine diagnostics are taken.

There are several ways that you can get involved.

- You can add data to our database by filling out our *Cases Analysis* form,
- you can support our studies by testing your clinically ill horse,
- you can provide feedback to your veterinary care provider,
- and veterinarians can request that our work gets a place at the next AAEP meeting to stimulate discussion. Open discussion is how science works.

Do you have a horse that has clinical signs and you are suspicious that it could be PNE? Fill out the form found at http://pathogenes.com/w/case-analysis/ . Our consultants are waiting to talk with you about your horse or your case.

If you have a clinically ill horse, don't guess, *test*! We don't have a Foundation; the revenue from testing supports our studies. You are probably unaware of the tremendous amount of money animal safety studies, effectiveness studies, and stability studies cost. It is not profitable for big pharmaceutical companies to do this work because revenue from Orphan disease won't cover the development costs. Compounding pharmacies do not do any of this work. Without your support the next life-saving treatment will go undeveloped.

Providing feedback to your veterinarian is important. Have those examinations after therapy and make sure a signed submission form is returned. Veterinarians see one to a few cases. Each case from a veterinarian that completed the paperwork becomes part of the database. This is very important as we move forward developing gene-based treatments.

And proactive veterinarians can move the discussion to the next level.

Your veterinarian may suspect or may have diagnosed PNE in your horse. And that means your horse may qualify for our study. The study is intended to satisfy several FDA requirements for licensing a treatment. The treatment must be the same used in all the horses in the study, the drug must have undergone rigorous testing and stability studies, and a target animal safety study must be completed using the exact same drug. It is important that you understand the study itself and what to expect. Polyneuritis equi is rare and there are no licensed treatments. This study is not placebo controlled and your horse doesn't need to have a cerebral spinal fluid analysis. There are forms to fill out and return. Your veterinarian is important, the forms must be completed and signed. If you are interested use this link: http://pathogenes.com/w/clinical-trial/

It was near Christmas 2012 when we met **Blue Eyed Playboy**. Blue was one of those cases you just don't forget.

The nightmare for his owner began in March of 2010, the veterinarian was summoned because Blue was stiff. Radiographs and vitamin E levels were normal. He was radiographed again in July and had a fluoroscopy in September. As costs for diagnostic tests increased, he continued to get worse. No cause for his clinical signs could be found. By March of 2011 he was admitted to Purdue. His clinical signs were hypermetria in his forelimbs and weak in the rear limbs. He would fall in his field. The working diagnosis was EPM although his "EPM panel" at UC Davis came back negative. The EPM treatment he was given didn't help him.

Over the next year he had his head, back and pelvis radiographed and injected, received a diagnosis of psoas injury, Lyme disease, and tested for PSSM. He had been back to Purdue in July 2012 with a complaint of "shifting leg" lameness. More diagnostics. More radiographs. Injections of ankles and feet didn't last. The Purdue clinicians determined he was weaker, more ataxic, and the hypermetric gait persisted. He was injected in both stifles and both sacral-iliac joints. Blue was failing. The prognosis was poor and euthanasia was recommended. But his family couldn't let him go.

In December of 2012 we tested Blue. He was negative for *S. neurona* antibodies but improved to almost normal using our recommendations. He "relapsed" 3 months later and again responded to treatment. Over the next 3 years Blue's owner would call and catch us up on his progress and discuss his relapses. He responded well to treatment and got back to trail riding--only to relapse again.

Why did he have chronic relapsing signs that would respond to treatment? He didn't have *S. neurona* encephalomyelitis, EPM. He was a conundrum for his veterinarian. He was a puzzle for Purdue clinicians. He was a frustration and heartache for his family. And for us he was a challenge, we knew we could alleviate signs for 3-12 months. And we knew we'd hear from his family again. This wasn't enough, we wanted to understand more.

Our database was invaluable because we identified 19 horses with similar histories. Eighteen of the 19 horses had been euthanized. Not surprisingly, the nineteenth horse succumbed a few months after our call. All this led us to *polyneuritis equi*.

Over the next few years we compiled data, made recombinant proteins, collected antibodies and mapped epitopes. We used these tools to understand and modify the ELISA test that was first published by Fordyce in 1987. We designed an algorithm and used it in our database to select a group of untreated horses that may fit with provisional diagnosis of PNE. A group of normal horses were also selected. Our algorithm predicted disease with uncanny accuracy just like those early cases identified by London researchers. Our findings were presented and discussed at the EPM society meeting and then published in the International Journal of Applied Research in Veterinary Medicine in 2015. It was interesting that as C reactive protein *increased* (a measure of inflammation) in these horses the statistical probability that the sample would contain antibodies against MPP would increase. We understand more about that today.

We last heard from Blue's folks in 2015. Life had been tough on the family and Blue's expenses hadn't helped. Our last memories of him are from a video we received. Blue's owner astride, he was peacefully ambling down a sunlit trail with birds singing in the background. This was prior to his last relapse. Had we known in 2012 what we know now I have no doubt we would report a different outcome for Blue. Blue's legacy is that others benefitted from his path. He made a difference. And it is likely your horse can too.

Diagnostics

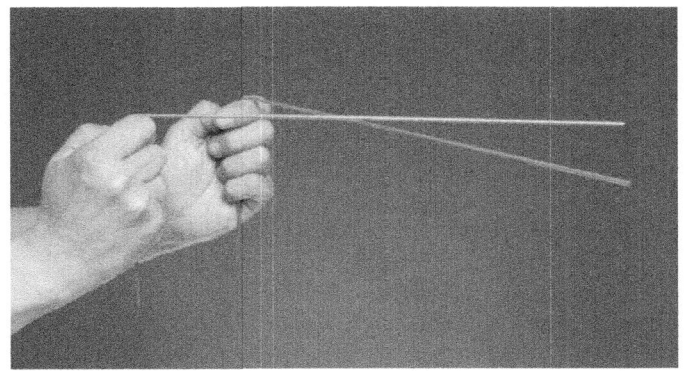

Testing Options

Polyneuritis equi

"It's not about what it is, it's about what it can become."
—Dr Seuss

We'd like to tell you we have a divining rod for polyneuritis equi (PNE). The fact is that there are some diseases that won't be diagnosed using a simple blood test. A classic example is equine protozoal myeloencephalitis (EPM). The organism thought to cause the disease, *S. neurona*, isn't often found in the brain or spinal tissues where the damage exists. When characteristic patterns of *inflammatory cells* are found on post mortem exam, the diagnosis of protozoal encephalomyelitis is assumed. We recognize EPM as a disease of inflammation.

Diagnosing EPM using IgG testing is akin to putting a square peg in a round hole. A refinement to testing serum for IgG was detecting IgG antibody in the cerebrospinal fluids, CSF. But that isn't definitive either. A further refinement to IgG-based disease detection: use the CSF: serum ratio and calculate a percent probability. The probability is correlated with a very few horses that did have disease.

A disconcerting finding with CSF testing for the detection of EPM was reported in the freedom of information summary for licensed EPM medications (NADA 141-188). We quote the results of positive testing: *"the CSF-positive test did not appear to be a major factor in determining treatment success nor a reliable measure of treatment success"*. We would like to develop tests that correlate with treatment outcome. A problem with EPM dogma is viewing an inflammatory disease through IgG-colored glasses. Sure, infection with *S. neurona* elicits an IgG response against *S. neurona*. A whopping 80% of horses in the U.S. get *S. neurona* infections and that results in a measurable IgG response. But only a tiny percent, 1% or less, of horses get EPM. Horses infected with *Sarcocystis* get an innate inflammatory response.

Polyneuritis equi is an inflammatory disease. And truth be told, eventually someone will make the link between *S. neurona* infections and polyneuritis equi. We do have tests that associate disease processes (pathogenesis) with PNE. The section *Research* explains the working hypothesis. PNE-diagnostics were developed in 1987. What was needed was some refinement.

Diagnostics are a major frustration for owners of neurologic horses. Owners may spend many hundreds of dollars on exclusionary diagnostics. Exclusionary diagnostics use tests to say what the disease is not. And still they may not have an answer at the end of it. Unfortunately, the nature diseases of the neurological system may require some exclusionary diagnostics. Some organisms trigger innate immune inflammatory cytokine responses that produce the clinical signs that are common to neurological diseases.

A horse can have *two active pathological processes!* The disease and the repair mechanisms (inflammation) that are associated with the disease. Disease and repair processes use similar pathways. This makes it unlikely that there will be definitive diagnostics for etiologies that cause PNE and the ability to separate diseases to the level of that etiology.

Our goal is selecting tests that correlate with treatment outcome. We kick the etiology can down the road. A short list of diseases starts with a good history and neurological examination by a veterinarian familiar with neurological disease and judicious use of diagnostic tests. The results of exam and testing will reveal a treatment protocol when PNE is suspected.

Polyneuritis equi is recognized by a set of clinical signs based on a few published cases and clinical experience. Neurologic deficits are seen in horses with abnormal gaits, changes in behavior or signs that are limited to the cranial nerves.

Here is the Clinical Scoring system we find useful:

Assigned Clinical Score: ***Enter the single value that best describes the clinical signs for each of the 6 categories below***: **0= no abnormal signs; 1=mild signs; 2=moderate signs; 3=severe signs**

Muscle tone: tongue tone, anus, perianal region, or urethral sphincter show decreased or absent muscle tone	CLINICAL SCORE
Sensitivity: Rubs tail; anal sphincter reflex decreased or decreased peri-anal region sensitivity; gluteal muscle, semitendinosus muscle, or semimembranosus muscle shows abnormal sensitivity; increased/decreased panniculus response	CLINICAL SCORE
Paresis or paralysis: Penis or urinary bladder resulting in abnormal urination or dribbling urine; masticatory muscles, facial muscle or tongue resulting in dysphagia or dropping feed; tail carried to one side; pelvic limb weakness resulting in mild ataxia	CLINICAL SCORE

Muscle atrophy or fasciculation: Top line decreased musculature; gluteal muscle, semitendinosus muscle, semimembranosus muscle, masticatory muscles, facial muscles atrophied or show fasciculations; fasciculation of supporting muscles when rear limb elevated; generalized muscle fasciculations	CLINICAL SCORE
Gait anomaly: Proprioceptive deficits, weakness on tail pull	CLINICAL SCORE
Cranial nerve signs: Abnormal behavior; vestibular nystagmus; head tilt or eye drop; asymmetric twist to lips	CLINICAL SCORE

As you can see the Clinical Score is an evaluation of 6 types of abnormalities in PNE. After treatment the Clinical Score is again determined. It is useful to circle the descriptor for each abnormality to evaluate the same parameters at each exam.

The chemical signaling mechanisms that microbes and animals use today is based on conserved, evolutionary successes. Redundancy is built into the chemical structures and even in the way signals reach the target tissues. Redundant molecules turn on *and* turn off these systems. Before I lose you, I am setting you up to understand the tests we are suggesting are going to be non-specific for etiology but useful for disease processes.

Signaling pathways are common to many tissues. An infectious agent will set off innate immune responses that are non-specific to a single agent. Vertebrates have many checks-and-balances (regulatory pathways) that control these common systems. Most of the time, everything works well. Yet, despite all the checks and balances, cytokine pathways can become *dysregulated*.

One inflammatory pathway that is appropriate to the discussion of PNE is cytokine IL6 (IL6), there are others. Cytokine IL6 is not as stable in specimens that are shipped through the mail. The result of IL6 stimulation is the production of C-reactive protein, CRP, is made by the liver. CRP is an acute phase protein. Acute phase proteins are found very early in infections. The levels of circulating CRP correlate with infections and resolution of inflammation associated with infections that results in a reduction of CRP.

Paradoxically, CRP is a stimulator of IL6. That means CRP turns on acute inflammation. Measuring CRP is circumstantial evidence of an infection due to bacteria, protozoa, or a virus. These infectious organisms stimulate IL6 production. The inflammatory pathway turns off when the infection is cleared. However, sometimes CRP doesn't signal the regulatory inflammatory cytokines to turn off, they keep the cycle going. The inflammatory response is dysregulated and results in chronic inflammation.

The CRP ELISA test returns a value in micrograms/ml and our target "normal" value is 16µg/ml. Most of the literature cites values measured in horses from tests that are less sensitive than ELISA testing. It is valuable to measure changes in CRP over time. In experiments we found that as the CRP increases it is more likely that inflammation has damaged the peripheral nerves and myelin has been exposed. When basic myelin protein 2, a myelin molecule found on the cytoplasmic side of cells that wrap nerve fibers, are exposed to the immune system antibody against myelin basic protein 2 (MP2) is produced. Healing by remyelination of nerve fibers restores function and the circulating MP2 antibody will go down. There is a highly reactive site on MP2, we call it MPP, that also stimulates an antibody response.

In rodent experiments, when disease becomes chronic the MP2 reactions abate while the MPP reactions continue. It may be similar in horses. We measure the levels of antibody against both proteins. Unlike the non-specific CRP molecule, antibody against myelin proteins indicates a disease state in which myelin is available to the immune system.

As we have previously stated: the overriding common factor in treatable PNE is the presence of antibody against myelin basic protein.

Any disease that exposes myelin will elicit antibody against myelin. Not every demyelinating neuropathy is PNE. However, the treatment approach may be useful in demyelinating scenarios.

To summarize our current approach, the PNE horse has evidence of neurologic disease that can be identified Clinical Signs. Most treatable cases have serum antibody against MP2. These are inclusionary criteria for our research studies.

The short list for neurologic diseases found in horses often do not have defining diagnostics. Excluding diseases may help define an etiology. A **diagnosis of exclusion** is a diagnosis of a medical condition reached by a process of elimination, which may be necessary if the etiology cannot be established with complete confidence from the history, examination or testing. Elimination of other reasonable possibilities is a major component in performing a differential diagnosis list.

The horse may or may not have antibodies against parasitic protozoa, but a good clinical exam should prioritize a presumptive diagnosis of EPM or PNE. Other exclusionary criteria are: no recent history of trauma, no recent respiratory infection (or a current vaccination for EHV-1 can satisfy this one). Vaccination for rabies will exclude rabies as a cause. Horses would have a normal serum vitamin E level ($> 1.5\ \mu/ml$).

Every horse is special to their owners. Each one is presented to us as the "horse of a life time". Their heart-horse. And they are special to us. This is Paddy, a thoroughbred stallion that was pastured with mares and the foals he sired. Such a special soul! He came too early in our studies but he lives on in our thoughts.

Made in the USA
Las Vegas, NV
05 January 2024